SECOND SPRING

A personal journey

ELLEN RUGEN

AMA BOOKS FRANCE ❤
2013

With thanks to the many Gers folk who were welcoming and helpful when I started to live there in 2005. Most names have been changed. I am of course responsible for my views and take on things.

Love and thanks to Keith Ross who made further adventuring possible.

ISBN 978-1-291-3921-7
Printed and distributed by Lulu Press.

CONTENTS

1

A click of the mouse

On September 2nd 2005 I flew to Pau, in South West France, collected a hire car and for the second time in my life drove on the right. An hour and a half later I arrived at Castelnau-Magnoac where I was to meet the *notaire*. I was about to become the proud owner of a village house some half an hour away in the Gers. An agent had taken me to it the previous April. I suppose I had spent all of twenty minutes to look it over. (Friends threw up their hands in horror and disbelief).

Despite appearances, I am not all that impulsive. I had not 'fallen in love' with the house. It is not by any stretch of the imagination idyllic. It's on a main road in a picturesque *bastide* village. As well as a sitting room, kitchen and two bedrooms, it has a basement, (street level at the back), garage-cum-cave-cum-deeply-interesting-space which I was able to fill with fantasies and possibilities. There is also a small yard. (I wanted some outdoor space not always available in a village house.) It was on target with my budget. Bingo!

It was some time before I made an offer. Back in the UK each morning I asked myself,

'Is it a Yes or a No? Am I going to make an offer or not?'
I knew that if my offer were accepted, I would go through with it. In the end it was a rather unsure:

'Yes if the price can be reduced'.
This left me a cushion to do the roof or repair whatever defects might need urgent attention. The offer was not immediately accepted but a few days later everything was set in motion without further ado. Whether it was because I was not having a mortgage (it was funded by a mortgage on my English flat), or whether because the French system is very clear cut, the only hiccup was that an English firm transferred my money to the wrong place and

in correcting it sent it twice over! The French side was patient but it could have been disastrous.

The house is constructed on heavy oak timbers (some still with the bark on), and mud. It has newish wiring and double glazed PVC windows and front door. It's cleanly decorated throughout with much of the walls covered in plasterboard giving a spic appearance and concealing whatever defects lie beneath. Having had some experience of surveyors reports before –

'We could not gain access to the floors as they were covered in carpet etc' I saw little point in employing a surveyor who would decline to comment on the very things that might give cause for concern.

The vendor was required to provide a survey on the presence of wood boring insects (of which there were many), and a termite report (of which there were none), and a lead survey of which there was a small amount. And so it was that the bi-lingual *notaire*, myself, the vendor, the estate agent and another *notaire* met in a beautiful oak panelled office in the square at Castelau-Magnoac and the various formalities were gone through and papers signed. The vendor then drove ahead of me to the house and explained how everything worked. I unpacked my sleeping bag, mattress and camping gas stove and settled down for my first night as a *propriétaire* on French soil. Voila!

'Why did you come?' I was often asked by French acquaintances. I started out with the usual fascination for all things French and this was further fuelled by several visits to a French friend who had bought a farm with half a hillside attached near Perpignan. She has a spectacular view of the Canigou mountain at the Eastern end of the Pyrenees. After a few trips out there I began to browse in estate agents' windows. But over the 18 months or so that I looked prices rose well beyond my budget except, I was told, for apartments in an old ski resort above Perpignan-Font Romeu. So I spent a few days in the resort out of season and saw shoebox apartments – two old ones and one newish one just within my price range. But did I want a shoebox apartment in a ski resort? As an investment which I would leave largely in the hands of agents to let out it would have done. But why not have an investment which I might actually like to stay in myself? So I turned to the internet and using one of the many property sites that cover the whole of France keyed in my budget of £40,000 and pressed 'anywhere'. It came up with a property near here. Right price and near the mountains. There was no way I could afford to take many exploratory trips. I flew to Pau, stayed in a B and B arranged by the agent, met quite a few people and returned 24 hours later. Whilst I was asking questions about an inaccessible wall, and the condition of the roof, the house was sold elsewhere. A few months later, I organised a second trip – four days this time – and saw a good range of properties including those with land that needed extensive renovation and a townhouse with an additional 'garage' some streets away which would itself have made a second property. Finally I asked to see this house which was in a local agent's window. It was in a village I had not been to. I thought the village very beautiful with its square and *columbage* houses (mediaeval wood and infill). The house though not wonderful had a good view out the back where there was also a little lane which made up for lack of grounds and promised rural strolls. I had already given up any idea of gaining land because I prioritised being near shops and not being dependent on a car. So after only that one viewing and a few questions I made the offer.

*   *   *   *   *   *   *

My locum post with the NHS finished the week before the completion date. I packed up the remains of my cupboard-cum-office; papers into boxes, files into other people's filing cabinets, some stuff to shred – not knowing whether I would need any of it again. The plan was to take a three month break from my family therapy work with the NHS – perhaps a little longer. It was my sixtieth year and although I was not ready to retire I could not but be aware of the time clock. I had tried to anticipate this milestone and watched with interest the routes taken by those who had gone before. Mine was in many ways a non-event. Nevertheless there were plenty of messages in the ether that I was unable to shrug off completely. Messages like 'Death can strike at any time' (both my parents were dead by 64)), 'Carpe Diem', 'Make hay while the sun shines', 'After 60 the brain begins to go, as does any part of the body you care to mention'. So the deal I struck with myself was: 'Fulfil some of my dreams at 60 so that when incapacity hits, I will not feel cheated or have a sense of regret that I passed up an opportunity to have time to myself and for myself.'

Thus I was choosing to participate somewhat belatedly in the live-life-to-the-full-now culture which my son subscribes to along with many a 20 year old. I was not to be, as someone succinctly put it, 'a 60 year old retiree' but 'a re-cycled teenager'. The plan was to return to work refreshed and pull together what had been a fragmented career incorporating as it did large chunks of time being a single parent and cobbling together part-time activities from caretaking to therapist, from cleaning to teaching. Not least it would be necessary I thought to get some more money in the bank whilst I could.

*   *   *   *   *   *   *

Where is the Gers? People look blank – 'never heard of it'. I go for Toulouse and qualify it with the Mid-Pyrenees. This conjures up a mistaken picture of mountains. When the light is right – which it was most of the days in that first autumn – the Pyrenees are indeed visible – a sort of fairytale sky line which is almost a cloudline. But the Gers is anything but mountainous. It is *vallloné* – gently undulating wooded ridges. The Roman roads or are they Napoleonic? (Or even Etruscan?) go straight at the ridges with some steep inclines and nothing in the way of hairpins. It has a reasonable amount of rain, plenty of sunshine and things grow fast. The colours are green for the fields and the forests, mellow red brown or cream for the houses. The Gers is agricultural – some vines, some cream coloured cows, and plenty of goose and duck flocks for the *foie gras*. In the summer the village becomes one large garden as veggies grow taller and fruitier than back home. A major picture postcard crop is sunflowers.

The Gersois, however, are not so much taken by this identity and refer instead to an earlier epoch when they were part of Gascony. People refer to those who originate from here – and it turns out not many do – as Gascoine. Gascony was English in the middle ages when Ailenore of Acquitaine married(?)Henry II King of England. The local dialect perhaps owes something to this occupation. Nasal sounds carefully cultivated in school French lessons are irrelevant here. Demain for example is pronounced demane and Monsieur Janvier, my neighbour, is pronounced, as spelt phonetically, with a short a. The area has from time immemorial been exposed to waves of immigrants such that the Gersois have a reputation of being open to strangers. The latest invasion of Brits, and to a lesser extent Germans and Dutch has brought them not a little wealth in that abandoned farmhouses, crumbling mud walls with their L shaped barns, have suddenly become a source of interest, renovation and speculation. So far this makes for an agreeable co-existence. The retirees are not competing in the job market and the families with young children have not yet swamped the schools. Most of us try to improve our French and it remains to be seen how feasible an enterprise this is for me.

My arrival story is perhaps more random than most though few people who have settled here seem to have begun with that specific intention. Not many retirees have researched different parts of France systematically and finally plumped for the Gers. One couple, however, started their search at Bordeaux and worked their way south finally taken by the combination of mountains and green. The area is still cheap for Brits. Lately the low cost airlines have been an added bonus for those who like lots of visitors or have reason to return to the UK. We are not reliant on the airlines – some people always drive whereas I like the high speed train and the option of a night in Paris.

2

Plumbing and Panic

My first visit was for little over a week and I planned to use it to prepare for the second visit the following month when I was going to drive over with possessions, tools, and a friend for moral support. My first experience of driving on the right hand side of the road had coincided with my earlier visit that year. Driving from A to B involved little more than negotiating the odd tractor and I wondered if I might not be gaining a false sense of confidence which would hardly hold up on the long drive around several major towns in a right hand drive English car going from one end of France to the other.

I decided to allow myself plenty of time to get used to things. In fact that first visit was dominated by two uncomfortable emotions – one was a series of panics as things didn't seem to work. I say 'seem to' because being in a state of panic, the fault was mainly mine though I still struggle with the front door key. That week I could only lock the door from the inside. In the end the estate agent came over with another key and a modus vivendi was established. I was not too much worried by leaving the door unlocked on my visits to the village for supplies – it seems a safe sort of place. But there is something very disempowering about not having control over one's front door.

The other feeling was unanticipated and was not so much about being on my own as about not moving here with my son who at the age of 20 was doing his own thing. It was the first time, I recalled, that I had moved to a new place without him. Pictures came flooding back of our two earlier moves together. In one we arrived before the furniture and camped in the smallest bedroom the first night – he was 6! Somehow being a mum always made me feel stronger and more powerful. A child's sense of wonder nicely dilutes any adult worries and fears. Thus it becomes a mute question – who is protecting whom? Whereas we have been separating over the last few years, that one week brought me to a point of grief and clarity. In that I think it was ultimately healing.

Another panic reduced me to paralysis when I couldn't turn off a powerful jet of water in the kitchen tap. This stretched my limited French to the limit. I rang the water board on my mobile and within five minutes a man arrived who I recognised as the man who had been working in the road that morning. He switched off the tap in the pavement and indicated that Monsieur R who lived beyond the church on the next corner was a plumber. After applying myself to several corners and quizzing passers by I found myself in the hardware shop where that morning I had bought what turned out to be a very expensive mop and various other cleaning things. Monsieur R had himself indicated that he thought it too expensive and to digress I find myself totally disarmed by the local disinclination to spin. The most shopkeepers will say is 'It's not bad' with a shrug and a pout. The estate agent remarked of

my very theatrically leaning roofs that
'They were certainly not new'.
Back to the water. I explained that I could manage without water for a day or so and would be very grateful if Monsieur R could see his way to coming the next day (or some attempt at this in French). The whole family came out to ponder the matter and it was decided that Monsieur R should come right away. Which he did and simply turned the tap off …. He also showed me which electrical switches turned the hot water boiler on and was disinclined to take much payment. I took some time to de-adrenalise. But as this type of misadventure recurs, I no longer panic. I trust more and more that things will work if I have more faith and that people will respond.

There has been a leak since – a real one this time – it turned out to be a very small hole in the mastic behind the shower. Water cascaded down the stairs to the *cave*. Monsieur R referred me elsewhere and the plumber came twice the next day; once to see what the matter was and a second time to mend it. When I asked him what I owed, he said he didn't know and to wait and see if the leak was fixed or not. Despite three messages to his answer machine, he has not replied – perhaps when he comes to plumb in my latest acquisition – a washing machine – he will add the two things together. I suspect not. This sort of gesture leads to a growing sense of security and confidence. (A dripping tap in England has not been fixed for a year now.)

I really was very much in the dark that first week. I started on the long haul of acquiring essentials, whilst maintaining little more than a campsite at base. I decided to venture into the nearest town by bus. I was not sure my navigational skills were up to town driving yet. And I was also keen to see how reliable the bus was. It was to the minute. My visit to Tarbes was partly driven by a need to get my mobile phone working with a French sim card. The mobile phone shop man was noticeably brusque and unsure whether his sim would be compatible. I walked around the main shopping street which was rather narrow and had a number of furniture shops in one of which I spied a chair on sale. Plucking up courage, I bought it and said I would return the next day to collect it in my car. I enjoyed the bus journey and was able to see much more than by car even though it was only a coach. I discovered LeClerc- first seen from the bus. (It's the big hypermarket chain.) The one this side of Tarbes is one of the smaller ones but still holds some furniture and appliances besides food. I splashed out and bought a folding bed which just about fitted into the car. It was not uncomfortable. My campsite was going upmarket.

At that stage, I was simply making things that much more manageable for myself. But it was not long before I faced the dilemma of who I was furnishing the place for. Was it for visitors? If so were they friends who were used to basic living or was it for paying guests or for letting the place out altogether? If I decided not to live there myself – I was after all just trying things out – should I be furnishing it at all? In other words a bit of an identity crisis loomed up quite early on and in some form or another continued throughout the year. Sometimes it was an undercurrent; sometimes it forced itself to the forefront and decisions had to be made.

That first week, I didn't make contact with the English community and particularly with Ted and Beth who had been so helpful when I was their overnight B and B guest earlier on in the year. Instead I started to meet the neighbours. The back of the house is a cul de sac but also a through walkway to the village shops. Consequently there is a lot of to-ing and fro-ing. One neighbour was a delight to meet. He spent much of the day when he was not in his garden which I understood was a little way away, interacting with his neighbours. Not much escaped his attention. He is however, unfortunately very deaf. What with that and my lack of language, our interactions were largely non-verbal. In a booming voice he would comment on what I was holding or doing,

'Ah vous avez un campagne!' (a brown baguette)

He might also comment on the weather. I would make a reply which was either inaudible or incomprehensible to him and he would say something else. There was something very comforting and reassuring about this kind of meeting. Other neighbours gave tomatoes or peaches and I felt welcomed. There were indeed questions about my husband. But once we established that I was alone that seemed acceptable. People drew their own conclusions.

I was keen to try out the village bar/restaurant which had a good reputation. People who were scarcely aware of Miélan had been to the Petite Marmite. More or less the first day I went there for lunch and assumed that they served evening meals. They did not. However, when I called in a second time, Joelle said that at the end of the week exceptionally there would be an evening meal as she had been asked to cook for a group. She was a little surprised that I was on my own but I was keen to have the meal anyway.

I turned up at the appointed time. The party had not arrived so I had an aperitif and then an English couple on holiday came by also expecting a meal. Joelle accommodated them and myself at separate tables, we got talking and ended up having an enjoyable time together. They were able to reassure me about driving down – it was their first visit and they thought it quite simple. Life stories were exchanged. It's impromptu meetings like this that I have always enjoyed most and feel most deprived of back in England where I tend to meet pretty much the same crowd. Whilst that makes for vintage relationships, it doesn't offer the excitement of the one-off no holes barred type of meeting. The food was generous, with multiple courses, beautifully cooked laced with wine during the meal and armagnac with the coffee – all for the grand price of 15 euros (£10).

I was, however, relieved to return to the familiar, or rather to get ready for my next trip to Canada for the birth of my first grandchild. When I looked back on that first week, I was very unsure how things would work out – indeed if they would. Had I taken on more than I could cope with and how long **would** those roofs hold out?

3

Settling in

A different journey in my loaded, elderly Golf, reinforced with a new clutch. I thought at the time:

'I will just be grateful if it makes the journey and lasts a month or two so that I can get to places to equip the house.'

The clutch after all only cost as much as a week's car hire. The crossing however was expensive – there are cheaper crossings but Plymouth to Roscoff is the most direct from Devon.

A friend offered to accompany me and I was grateful for the support though her eyesight prevented her from helping with navigation. She brought with her a weighty bag which meant I had to leave some of my stuff out. I often find these sort of compromises make for tricky travelling a deux and whether from impatience or resignation, I end up travelling alone.

I arranged to spend the first night with a friend in Britanny. We reached her after a three hour drive by which time I had more of a sense of driving on the right and the headlamps had been tried out in a misty sort of day with their bits of plastic glued on heaven knows which way to deter them from shining into the oncoming traffic. But did they really? And how do you know where exactly to put them when all the accompanying diagrams bear no resemblance to the plain round headlamps we had?

I was keen to see her set-up. She had moved the previous month lock stock and barrel. Consequently she had a largish well-appointed fully equipped, functioning house with a couple of hectares of land ringed with prolific chestnut trees. There was ample space for her to pursue her love of gardening. Her main concern was her cat. Indeed he had been the deciding factor in location. She felt he couldn't manage a longer journey from the ferry and although she might have liked to be further south and warmer, the cat's welfare was paramount.

How to manage pets is an ongoing concern for those of us with pet attachments and wanting to switch countries. My decision for the time being was to leave my cat in England with my son in charge until my return at the beginning of the winter. This revolving door tides me over for the first year when I shall think again. It makes for a joyous reunion when I return and some sadness as I depart. I like to think that he can inveigle those around him to give him the affection he deserves – the cat that is. Other people are quite happy to go travelling with their cats albeit in a large rabbit cage taking up all the back seat. I was sure my car phobic cat could never cope with that – he is after all nearly 18 or 116 in human years.

The next day was the long haul. We went almost entirely on the auto routes and made it by late evening with a longish stop in Lectoure late afternoon. Lectoure was one of those unplanned discoveries. I stopped at a not particularly interesting café on a not particularly interesting road and we went for a stroll only to find ourselves in a thriving historic place with a huge church cum Cathedral on one of the de Compostella routes. The town was heaving with people: at the bottom of the main road were thermal baths.

The house was a little more familiar this time and none the worse for being left for a month. Friend bravely coped with camping facilities a bit stretched to provide for two. Outside the front door, was a new little blue enamel number plate – 37. The whole village had sprouted number plates like this in the month I was away. Apart from always hankering for a French blue plate (for my English flat!), it gave me a good feeling about being part of a community with a Mairie who made such communal decisions. Practically it made organising visits by tradesman, indeed by anyone, much easier. My road must have had some 80-100 residents and all were simply listed by name so that my address hitherto had been my name followed by the name of the road. The inference that the post office must know each of us by name had also signified to me something of a sense of intimacy and inclusion.

I had plenty of time to get down to further business so we took a day trip to the Pyrenees a little over an hour's drive away. It was in-between seasons and very quiet. Arreau was hemmed in by steep sides and noticeably cooler and dour. I refused to tackle the hairpins a higher run would have meant so we strolled and sat by the river. It was not unlike Dartmoor, however, very unlike the Gers where rivers are few and those that do exist are often opaque and motionless. I found myself glad to get back to the mellow creams and rust-red roofs of the Gers compared with the grey stone and steep rooves of the Haute Pyrenees.

A few days later after further sorties to get some sort of phone connection and a possible source of secondhand furniture I drove my friend to the airport and faced a stretch of time alone with plenty to do without the pressure of any deadlines. I had planned to return to Devon around the 1st December. This fitted in well with three rhythms; - my son was leaving for work and snowboarding in the Alps around that time – this meant his room would be free (I had let out my room), the cat needed looking after and, it would be getting cold here. I was fairly certain that the house did not have adequate heating or insulation for the winter months. Moreover I thought that two months was the most I could manage of this pioneering life style. Finally, and incorrectly as it turned out, I understood that a job near Oxford was becoming available at that time and those I had worked with were keen that I should apply for it.

The plan threatened to be overturned when I was invited to attend an interview for another post in Bristol in the middle of November. This led to some soul-searching not least because I didn't feel I should have been offered the interview since I was asked to present aspects of my research when research was not anything I had done for some years as indicated on my application. I was suspicious that I had been invited simply to keep up the numbers or to show a political correctness in inviting someone who was 60. Did I want to disrupt *my* plan which after all was simply a matter of personal convenience for such a long shot of a post? In the end I decided that I would attend the interview but that I would return to France for the last two weeks as intended. I would make use of the interview to return home very briefly, to pick up papers which I needed for my presentation, do one or two things in Bristol and break up my rather isolated existence here. Meanwhile I heard that the Oxford post was postponed to be re-advertised 'in due course'.

*   *   *   *   *   *   *

I became quite cat-like. I wanted to explore every nook and cranny, sniff the air, and gaze at the Pyrenees. I went out for long lingering walks in all directions and carefully retraced my steps guided by the Miélan church spire. I also went out in the car – usually no more than an hour's drive and usually with some purpose such as a search for further supplies. At other times I curled up and slept or read and gradually began the discipline of writing a film script.

The road to the side of the house trails off into a lane little used by cars. It's a very fertile lane and I like to go out at dusk and watch the bats. There is a turn off next to a large house; a fig tree laden with fruit seems to belong to nobody on the edge of a field; the tarmac changes into a path. An enclosure of pheasants being reared for the hunt follows on one side and on the other there are very large vegetable and fruit gardens – each is about the size of three allotments making a good oblong stretch of land. (I found out later that one of them belonged to my elderly neighbour.) The track becomes a path with a wildflower meadow to one side leading on to endless woods. A caravan straddles the path and I have not gone further.

There's a walk on a turning off the lane further down with yellow signifiers at intervals. This walk continues on a rise of woodland and then drops down through the woods to the edge of cultivated fields. But the initial back lane itself is full of surprises apart from the shrill little guard dogs who announce my coming. One evening I walked into the edge of my favourite field because there can be a view of the mountains when they are clear. It was twilight and an animal I took to be a deer came bounding over. It stopped within a few feet, sniffed and waited for a couple of minutes. It was a large hare and a magical moment. More sadly another time there was a beautiful barn owl lying on the bank – presumably hit by a car. It had a thick outer coat of white feathers.

On the other side of the main road, less than a mile away is a large lake. The land in that direction is farmed and criss-crossed with farm tracks many of which I explored in a foraging way. I know where there's mint, fennel, cherries, walnuts, chestnuts, spinach, chives and some lesser known salad items. Although this area is sparsely wooded there are some great trees by the sides of the tracks.

I was hesitant at first not knowing how public these paths were. Every so often there is a small herd of creamy cows and there are chickens near the farms and a few industrial agricultural looking sheds. But mostly there is just space with views to the next wooded ridge. The lake was looking very sorry for itself after an exceptionally hot summer. This meant that large areas of it at one end could be simply walked across. There was something a little sinister about the tall plants and creepered trees where water should be and I was glad to find the edge with a mixture of pines and other trees.

Most walks in that direction inevitably led to a beer at the Hotel du Lac. This is a unique establishment – a cross between a motel, a campsite and a small-holding. The outside, which is the best place to be, offers a view of the lake and various inquisitive fowl activities. The chickens mate and kick up dust baths next to the plastic tables: the geese come and occasionally stretch out their necks to investigate a trousered leg. One is also surrounded by ex-agricultural carts and implements for ornamental purposes? Table tennis tables and several amusement arcade machines are not far away. There are great flourishing pines, weeping willows and banana palms side by side in this climate which is both Mediterranean and Pyrenean. As it was not the season there was rarely more than one other person or group there at the same time and the whole eclectic combo meant stopping here was one of my treats.

I was surprised one time I was hanging out there to find that the waitress who I had taken for French was in fact from Newcastle. She explained that she was a *saisonnière* working in the ski resorts in the winter. She had come to visit a friend in Miélan and much preferred the laid-back ambience to her existing summer job on the Mediterranean coast. This job was vacant and so she had reinstalled herself here with another month of working before visiting her parents who lived elsewhere in France whilst she waited for the Alpine season to begin again.

Making contact with Ted and Beth again meant that I was somewhat taken in hand. Beth kindly fitted a guided trip to one or two secondhand furniture stores near Tarbes some three quarters of an hour away into her otherwise busy life. They run a *Gite, Chambre d'hôte,* four dogs, a horse and are engaged in an ambitious building programme providing something of a barn-cum-leisure centre in the midst of a fertile agricultural valley. I came away from the furniture store having found two beds to be delivered in two weeks time and with other possible items to brood upon. As I have mentioned before I was very unclear about what or whom I was furnishing for. To play safe, I was only buying essentials. I was also very unclear about my funds. Did the roof need extensive repairs? Was I about to get a well-paid job? I did a quick calculation and worked out that I could provide basic facilities for about £800. This was far more than I would have spent in England where I always buy things second hand. But here second hand didn't seem what people did. I couldn't quite understand this since there seemed a regular traffic of English people migrating and returning. Some people ship things out from the UK: others sell up entirely and buy their houses fully furnished from an English vendor. Buying mostly from new therefore involved shopping around and the shop I knew would have the most reasonable stuff was IKEA in Toulouse two hours drive away. But I was not ready for that length of trip yet.

3

Getting hold of people

Although there's a flourishing Brits community in Trie, 10 miles south and in Marciac and Tillac about the same distance North and even I suspect in Mirande about the same distance East, I did not meet any Brits in Miélan. Because Ted and Beth are the mainstay of the Trie group and maintain a sort of email information service as well as promoting Quiz nights in the Café de Sports, I tagged on to this group which meets regularly for coffee on a Tuesday morning. However ambivalent I am about creating a Little Britain out here, this community is an invaluable source of information, support and gossip centring on main family events such as births, marriages and deaths and how to fill in tax forms.

With my poor French, my contact with French people who had little or no English, was always going to be limited so French classes were a big priority. By happenstance, an Englishman seeing my GB car made contact and although he himself was on holiday, he put me in touch with two other people one of whom moved to the area with her family a year ago and is in the same line of business – a psychologist. She recommended her French class some 12 miles away

The French class is the highlight of the week. It's not only the class which has at most four participants, and the energetic and charming way Nadège teaches, but also the view. Montesquieu approached from the plains is a striking mound with ramparts as its name suggests and the premises look out over a far vista. We have not yet made it to the *auberge* after class where we understand the food is very good. I was disappointed to find there were two week half term breaks after my first class so I was only able to attend three classes before my December return.

After that first class I felt a surge of confidence – it was a delight to be able to try to speak French and to know that I would be understood and corrected. The class is entirely in French and Nadège expresses the meaning of words by actions and gestures. New vocabulary, new expressions, hit my notebook by the minute. Other times however, I feel weighed down by how little I know with awareness of how much there is yet to learn and my limited powers to do that at my age.

I also joined a 'Stretching' class. This would, I hoped, enable me to meet local women besides keeping up a bit of the Yoga I do in England. Again the class turned out to be delightful. I was amused by it all and I think they were amused by me. The teacher shouts out 'very good' every now and then but more often comes over to give instructions somewhat impatiently as I mistake *talons* for hands (they are heels) and stretch when I am supposed to be bending knees or whatever. In time I introduced Patricia, my newly acquired psychologist friend, to the class and she in turn brought along another young English mother. But the star of the class is Ninette, the organiser. We thought she said her age was 76

– I was never quite sure – we had taken her as being late 50's. She does two classes a week and manages all the positions. I certainly don't feel out of place on account of my age.

I had plenty of spare time especially in the evenings. This proved to be the best time to write though sometimes I had my nose in a book. Quite how the beginning emerged I cannot recall. I had been to a workshop on writing film scripts and I wanted to try my hand at this as I do conceptualise things in a visual way. I think I had the first scene from my visit to Ottawa's Modern art gallery and it all developed from there. I was very aware it was a first attempt and that I was following my family's life story uncomfortably closely. But I also wanted to make a point or two, educationist as I am. There was an irresistible theme in my own life of an unfulfilled love spanning many years: giving this some meaning and space satisfied something deep within myself. It also changed my external perception of it and I think helped me to 'cut the ties that bind'. Whether it works or not as a film script I have yet to see. But I have long learnt to enjoy the process of writing with not too much investment in the result.

Synchronistically one of the novels I was reading was about a number of characters who loved each other but because of different life circumstances could not be together. There was also a blind character and as some of my recent work has been with the blind I wanted to have someone speak about the process of going blind – something I have seen little of in fiction.

I had long earmarked this time as when I would try to write. It is something I have had a stab at over the years but never it seemed found the right conditions – as Virginia Woolf put it – a room of one's own and £500 per year. Now I had these conditions and it might only be for a short time. Thus it was all the more frustrating when days passed without writing. In this I turned to 'The art of creativity' by Julia Cameron. This is a self-help guide to blocked creativity and employs a prescriptive style which though it makes me bridle at one level, never left me without some insight as to what the problem was or what I might do to get going again. Once I had the main idea and characters, I found dialogue came effortlessly and I soon had the end but not what lay between. The script was well on its way before my return to England when I went for a tutorial with the workshop teacher. She gave me guidelines about what to change and I went on to finish the first draft during the English winter evenings.

It was getting cold in the evenings. In November the autumn days could still be like an English summer except that the trees were beginning to look bare. I noticed my neighbour bringing a tractor stacked up with wood on several occasions and asked him if he would bring wood for me. The front room has an unattractive heap of a metal box with a few dents and a door which didn't close – a *cuisinière*. The agent had commented when she had shown me round

'Well you'll have to get rid of that!'
New stoves it seemed were around the £1000 mark. Most done up farmhouses have new stoves but no-one seemed to think they give out much heat – of course their converted rooms were much bigger than mine. I had fond memories of a small Swedish fire which had belted out heat in another house I have lived in. Either way it seemed a large expense was on the cards and I was not even staying for this winter. Ted, however, came to the rescue: he

was interested in getting the existing one going and came to fiddle with it. It clearly needed new linings and I was instructed to get these from the hardware store. The oven door was never going to work but that didn't matter. So fingers crossed after the chimney sweep had given the go-ahead, I lit my first fire and ran outside to make sure smoke was emerging. The fire was as the neighbour remarked a lot of work. For the few weeks I had the fire it was a novelty not without a panic or two. Once some wood I had put to 'warm up' in the oven self ignited and flames rushed out merrily as I let in air on opening the door. As the house is made of timber and mud, I remained in awe of the fire and it was as much a worry as a comfort at times.

Snow began to appear on the mountains and were an enticing sight when I looked out of the front door each morning. I longed to get up there. Patricia gamely agreed to accompany me, en famille, and so one weekend we headed up just before the end of November. Her youngest's car seat, the two older children and husband filled one car so I went in mine. Neither of us had encountered the winter mountain roads before and it was not long before we realised that we lacked the necessary kit. Chains were available at considerable expense in a wayside garage. I parked my car and we all squashed into theirs with chains. (Had we known, the roads were due to be cleared the following week.) Uncleared, the roads were extremely hazardous, however, we were determined to get there as best we could. By the time we arrived at La Mongie we were shaking. A café was open but the resort as a whole was not. Buried cars on either side were an impressive sight. After a coffee we waded out with the toboggans we had brought before facing the return journey. Driving back down it seemed there was only a hair's breadth between us and the sheer, white, valley below.

I never did manage to find out the condition of the roof timbers, although getting them inspected had been my priority on arrival. There had clearly been a leak the previous winter – stains on the wallpaper in the back bedroom. I was keen to have preventative work done if necessary. My meetings with builders, however, were not a great success. I first applied to a builder with a prominent office in the main square. This was it seemed quite a large outfit and two well-dressed men came – the proprietor and his partner who had more English. They proposed to get two men (for safety reasons) out for a days work replacing any cracked tiles at a cost of not more than 800 euros. It was difficult to know what to do: on the one hand it seemed excessive since there might be very little work to do: on the other I was reluctant to pit my lack of expertise against theirs. There was another encounter in the office where the proprietor said that he had too much work on but he could just let me have three men the following day between jobs at a cost of 1,800 euros! That office disappeared soon afterwards.

I turned to an English builder who came in due course with an outside ladder but not an inside ladder. He gave me a verbal and later a written estimate for doing as he put it small repairs which because of awkward accessibility were quite costly. In the end I let things be and followed his other advice which is with these very old roofs,

'You just wait until there's a leak and then do something about it'.

I would have liked to have a look at the roof

timbers myself but the access was right above the stairwell and difficult to get into. One morning however, I happened to go upstairs when the sun was in a certain position which illuminated the roof space. I could see some wonderfully bent timbers. It was to be another year before I got up there myself or got hold of a reliable French builder.

When the time came to pack up, I left the car in the basement turned off the electricity and water and made my way slowly to Pau airport with a streaming cold and a well-worked out combination of bus, train and airport shuttle.

Had I made the right move? I wasn't at all sure. I looked forward to a snug gas centrally heated winter, seeing off my son to the Alps, entertaining, and finding some temporary work to tide me over to a 'proper job' or my miniscule pension the following April.

4

The first spring

Friends not infrequently remarked on my courage or said things like,

    'I couldn't possibly do what you're doing!'

Flattering though this was to the ego, it didn't mean all that much to me. I was doing what I was doing. However, much as I dreamed of 'my little place in France' during the long English winter, there was some reluctance to return to something of nothingness at the beginning of April. This was compounded by having an all too brief a time with my daughter and grandson who were visiting from Canada about the time I had planned to come back. So leaving my cat with a series of temporary sitters until my son returned at the end of the month and leaving the safe environment of my

English home, there **was** a point where some courage was needed. I treated this fear gently with the promise that I could return a month later for a few days to meet my son whilst my return rail ticket was still valid.

I was doing it by train this time with a stopover in Paris where I have a friend I see every five years or so. Travel proceeded uneventfully although the hotel I thought I had booked had cancelled my booking as they had not received my confirmation letter. I had a particularly heavy suitcase which I wheeled across the street from the Gare du Nord where virtually every building is a hotel. The first was expensive but in the bar of the second one, grandmama was doing her ironing and the whole reeked of bygone days. Yes they had a room up some dusty stairs and along an ill-lit corridor. The room itself was large with its own bathroom and reasonable at 40 euros.

The following day I travelled south for 6 hours. The trees began to unfurl until they were fully out after the Landes. Sitting across the aisle was a passenger with a small white cat in a basket on the table. This gave me ideas.

Arriving back in the evening, I was almost surprised to find that nothing had changed. The roof had not leaked and there was no smell of damp. In fact the house had been aired by way of the open hatch to the roof. The car in the basement was a bit mouldy inside and did not immediately start. The next day I rang my English breakdown service and within half an hour, the local garage man appeared, got the car going and drove off to check it over.

I immediately got into driving. I hadn't driven for a long time and the joy of everything working made me take-off. I took off to the Pyrenees in search of snow and a possible late ski. I ended up walking by a river with snowy mountains ahead. I took off to IKEA – a two hour drive away on rural roads. I came out of IKEA with lots of little things to make the house more of a home. I also arranged for a new couch and chair to be delivered. I have only once had a new couch before and feel quite possessive and protective of its cream cover. I was welcomed back to the stretch class and to the French class and voila – my minimal structure for the week was in place.

The only problem was with France Telecom. My telephone had been cut off as a result of bills not being paid or received in my absence. I thought I had arranged for the phone to be cut off – hence when a solicitor's letter arrived the next day I was put out to say the least. It was several weeks before this got sorted. This delayed my attempting to research the possibility of teaching English privately in the village since I had no contact phone number. Some weeks later and some 200 euros poorer I had a landline once again and my home was established as a *residence secondaire* which meant that I was entitled to cut off and resume my telephone line up to six times a year without paying reconnection charges.

Aside from essentials, I felt myself expanding in tune with the leaves. The first few days were very bright and sunny before one colder day. It felt like late spring. So much had come out. I had jumped a month or two. Some days were more typical of an English summer. I put a heater on in the evenings not more than three times.

My French neighbours resumed friendly and polite greetings. I crossed paths more often with the men than with their wives so I was especially glad when I met Madame M in the back lane. She was carrying her compost to the garden and we exchanged essential details such as how many children we had and where they were, and about her health – she pulled a face – she walks in a laboured way with a stick. She then invited me to her garden. This turned out to be one I had admired before on my evening strolls. I had a guided tour past the flowers and the vegetables, into the little den-come-cottage which has a bed, water, and a stove. Round the back there is a shaded area of grass round the blue pine which is now impressively tall and which she planted 25 years ago. There is a wisteria arch and nearby some plants which caused us to deliberate about the name - *monnaie de pape*. Madame mimed the pope until I got it. Then I was slow to get something flat and transparent – like money. Ah yes, the penny dropped- it was Honesty in English. Madame told me that she had been born in Venice but Monsieur was a Gascoigne. I wonder where they met – during the war perhaps? They have two sons, one living in Bordeaux and the other in a different area. I wonder are they Protestant or Catholic and hope that in time my French will improve enough to have a fuller conversation. I turned down the offer of a bouquet of tamarind. The fine spray of pink trees was everywhere. But no I was setting off for England in two days time and it would be a waste.

The temperatures were not too different at the airports. As I travelled into London, I went back a month or two. White blossom from the hawthorn bushes was everywhere. The trees were just beginning to come out. It was early spring here, my second spring.

The quick trip home allowed me to catch up on some of the snowboarding sagas, and be around whilst my son picked up the threads of his life. He was able almost immediately to get back to his summer job of the previous year and hoped to improve his income by getting into building work. Fortuitously amongst my most recent mail was a letter inviting me to an interview on one of my four days in England. Not so fortuitously, I heard from the director after my return to France, that he had been called out to an emergency meeting of the NHS Trust at which it was decided to freeze all new posts due to a financial crisis following government stipulations that the NHS trust was overspent. He gave feedback on the interview: - the gist of it was that I did not have quite enough experience. This caused some soul searching and with some angst I decided that I would have to give up the search. When there are NHS funding difficulties, mental health and the elderly services suffer most. It was unlikely therefore that there would be posts advertised in the next few months, so I was not going to get the more experience required, nor could I afford the professional fees, or the travel expenses or general wear and tear of chasing what might only be shadows. Effectively I have come to the end of that road and frustratingly am retired professionally whilst feeling at my most skilled. As well as a feeling of loss, however, there are things I am glad to leave behind – the stress of working in a large organisation driven by economics but with rhetoric suggesting the primacy of patient care. It was only after I had made that decision that I realised what a strain it had been keeping that option open whilst pursuing settling into life in France. One of the luxuries of 'retirement' is that I can single rather than multi-task. I take delight in seeing processes through with few interruptions. And I have time to write.

Thinking beyond my immediate situation, though, therapeutic services which are organisationally tied in with medical services are bound to lose out. In the multi-disciplinary teams I have been in, the psychiatric input has swallowed a disproportionate amount of resources and maintained an inappropriate hierarchical authority. My limited experience of family therapy in France is that it is provided in the community and may maintain a greater autonomy. On a bigger scale, NHS Trusts have to balance changing government policies, patients' acute life-threatening needs with less definable therapeutic needs. Does the high profile case of a woman claiming her right to Herceptin, (a cancer drug) mean that a family therapy post has been cut? Of course it is fanciful to suggest there is a direct link, but the Trust is the same as the one I applied to.

*   *   *   *   *   *   *

I expected that friends would be keen to come out and have a look and a bit of a holiday. Hence I made sure there were spare beds and bedding and issued invitations to all and sundry. After four prospective visitors made other arrangements for one reason or another, I dropped that expectation. When I thought about what I wanted, it was people close by who were into sharing trips or would enjoy going to the odd event. Soon after I had this thought, I met Maggie.

I had known about the arrival of Maggie and been briefly introduced to her. I met her one Sunday when I was rounding the corner to my car to set off to a *vide grenier* in another village.

'What a great idea' she said. 'We'll go in my car because I've got Bessie'.
Bessie is a large and lanky black dog – part Great Dane and part something else.

It was an especially bright morning, not too hot and the best *vide grenier* I've been to. The village which we explored later had a distant vista and a viewpoint which was on the *Compostella* way. We exchanged some of our life story and hoped that this meeting and outing would be one of many.

Maggie was about my age and has bought a large villa a few doors down the street. It has a corner plot of land and as we sat under the shady trees, I remarked that I could imagine we were in the West Indies where she had been brought up. She refers to it as her park. The house has not been occupied for twenty years and Maggie is determined to get it totally renovated in three months but nevertheless we managed an outing to a Brazilian do.

It was an outside event in a small patio area at the back of a gallery and café. The three piece band with singer was close and intimate. The star turn was the appearance of a gorgeous dancer clad luxuriantly in gold draped material, with golden skin seductively revealed and crowned with tall headgear to match. Her enthusiastic and graceful invitation to all and sundry to dance was quite bewitching. Soon even the most inhibited Brit was swaying unexpectedly rhythmically though the Gersois, it was noted in the paper the next week, were more timid.

Maggie was very focused on supervising the works to her house and I fell back on my own company with a growing expectation that I would meet one or two acquaintances anyway and that come my next visit Maggie would be a possible playmate from time to time.

In June I had my first visitor. The friend who had accompanied me on the journey down at the beginning called in as she continued a tour of France. She was camping, hostelling and meeting up with friends. I was pleased to see her and a little curious how it would be to have a visitor after all this time. We did one tourist thing and drove an hour north to a major Gers monument. The Cistercian abbey is now a state designated ancient monument which houses a donated art collection with a Cézanne a Van Gogh and some Rodin sculptures amongst other works. The atmosphere of the monastery was very serene and simple. I could imagine living there and sensed the contemplative vibe. My own version of the contemplative day to day was, however, necessarily suspended: I felt increasingly overwhelmed watching my living-room-cum-study become the site of a of camping holiday sort-out. It was not the easiest of visits and something of a lesson about needing to make some boundaries. Another tension was that my friend had little interest in meeting or having anything to do with the French. I had already arranged to attend the annual dinner of the stretching class to which Ninette had warmly invited my friend. Friend attended reluctantly but I puzzled over our different priorities, and perhaps fears. In doing so, I became more aware of my own values, and my appreciation of local acceptance and generosity. I could say, many people round here seem to operate 'from the heart'. My instinct is to trust, which spares me from the constant drain of weighing up of options and costs.

One good friend rang from time to time to see how I was getting along. It caused me to question other friendships. Surely I would have checked up on them if they were starting out on something new. I rang one and sent an email birthday greeting to another. I concluded that the hectic pace at which my friends live even in rural Devon means that being away for two or three months is barely noticeable and that my sense of it being a significant time is just different. On the other hand, I never know when I live somewhere and then move on, which friends were in retrospect only of that time and place and which few precious ones will stay for life.

I had another guest – a cat. This gorgeous silky grey was booked into a cattery whilst its owners went on a three week holiday. I could not resist. On my first visit to her home the cat made a beeline for me and snuggled into my neck. I kept an eye on Blossom and she kept an eye on me. I got up much earlier and more regularly than usual, got far more writing done and was less inclined to make spur of the moment decisions to go out for the whole day. In the longterm this would have been restricting but in the short term it was grounding. There was a downside in that after a week or so it was apparent that the flea collar was not doing its job. Fleas make me feel so powerless. I also am not fond of chemicals. However, flea management is part and parcel of having cats so I improvised with lots of washing, some chemicals and grinning and bearing it until her owners returned. Blossom was curious and although I think after a week or so she would not have run away, I kept her on her harness when she was outside in the little yard. Mostly she slept inside and would have loved to spend the night in my bed but that was definitely out.

May continued with days of sunshine alternating with rain, and even, one evening, hailstones. One week was brilliantly hot in the day followed by spectacular thunderstorms in the evening and night. This happened three days and nights running and sparked a growth spurt. When I went on one of my regular walks I was festooned with so many wildflowers, including orchids, bushes in flower, climbing scented roses that I thought for a moment I was on an acid trip. After several dry days and a grasscutter, this ephemeral display had all but vanished.

I continued to acquire possessions mainly with the possibility of letting the place for the two months I was away in the summer. Patricia, who was proving to be a great support and friend, had lent me a comfortable armchair which nicely supplemented my IKEA clic clac couch in the sitting room. Other friends supplied a cottage style table and chairs which were stabled in their garage 'Better off for being aired' they said. A friend remarked that there would have to be a washing machine. The next day one appeared! In my evening strolls I had noticed on the shuttered window of a private house a poster announcing a one day sale of furniture the following Monday. I showed up and after the usual fumbled greeting in French found out that Ken was returning to the UK in two days time and his household furniture which he had shipped out from England three years before was not going to be shipped back. Did he have a washing machine – yes. I took on several other small bits, shelving, duvets etc. Whilst looking round I met an English couple who had a *chambre d'hote* and *gite* on the edge of Miélan. We agreed that it would be good to meet up as neither of us had met English people before in Miélan.

There were *vide greniers*- or carboot type sales dotted around the area. These were a playground for me – I picked up odd things like a French monopoly set, a blue electric kettle and one or two more ancient ornaments. And so my little place became more of a home – my home.

There was one extravagance. Le Clerc was selling an array of summer garden furniture including a *balancelle*. This is a swinging couch – I don't know the name in English but it is something I have always hankered after. The box fitted in the car and with some difficulty I assembled it. At 69 euros it was less than £50! I set it up in the garage looking out on the tomatoes, aubergines and pansies – my portable garden growing on the sunnier side of my backyard.

5

Entente cordiale

Monsieur C, it was announced was giving a lecture on Anglo-French relations in the Hundred Years War in the Monastere des Carmes, Trie. It would be in French with an English translation and there was a meal afterwards consisting of *garbure,* (a local speciality) and creme *anglaise* (custard). I went for the lecture but declined the meal as I felt obliged to keep my newly arrived guest – the cat – company. I was not also sure about the menu, though as our hostess for the evening explained many more delicacies had been donated by local suppliers – too many to be put on the poster.

Monsieur C delivered a tour de force. Declining a microphone, he used the acoustics of the church to enact, mime and passionately indicate the depth of his subject and thus facilitate understanding to his (mainly English) audience. The translator whether through shyness or ineptitude declined to translate unless prompted by the chairwoman. She asked us to put up our hands if there was anything we did not understand- and no-one did (either). I was pleasantly surprised to find that I got the gist. This was based on a complicated set of royal marriages interweaving the French with the English. Confusion came to a head when there was not a straight male successor to .... whereupon the mainly English line came into conflict with another branch of the family and war broke out. There were two heroic characters in the story – the Black Prince who was quite dominant in this area and Febus, a hero of the Basque next door, who managed to avoid deferring to either side. Monsieur C did not confine himself to the 100 years war period, and brought a conflict between Napoleon and Wellington to life when he handed round shot dug up from the site of a battle in the Gers. He spoke of the writings of Arthur Young in his survey of the Pyrenees. The heart warming theme was that we are one family and that there has always been a strong connection between the British and the French in this area particularly. I came away feeling enthused about this 'performance-type' presentation of history and that I belonged here (although my ancestry is somewhere Spanish Jewish and somewhere German and only in the last 200 years or so English!)

Neighbourly relations continued to be firmed up when Madame M knocked on the door one day with a huge bag of cherries. Two days later Monsieur M did likewise and whilst thanking him I tried to explain that Madame had already given me some. Cherries continued abundantly through the rest of May and June. There are it seems very many varieties fruiting at different times. The little wild cherries are especially delicious. At times I even felt cherried out.

I was able to reciprocate in some way when my visitor came with a store of oats; she made three batches of flapjacks, one of which was for the neighbours.

6

Preparing for the summer

As time came near to returning to England for July and August, things speeded up: there was a comfortable time with more to do and less time to fill or make decisions about. As usual I was caught in pursuing several paths at once even though I had let the professional path go. I was very unsure whether the house would be let out. This meant I had to prepare the house in case. I embarked on a quick lesson from Ted as to how to connect up light fittings. For various reasons it was not that simple and I kept popping in to Madame in the electrical shop for this and that. When I asked if she had the right sized screw driver (I meant for sale), she gave me hers and asked me to bring it back the next day.   Whether because this was a better balance of doing and being or whether I had simply become more part of the place as I got to know more French people I cannot say. But I would be missing out part of the story if I did not admit to lows. These were days which I have some amnesia about. At worst, they were once or twice a week and they were days when nothing was arranged and equally I could not get up any enthusiasm to do anything. They are a hazard of being on one's own. On balance I value for now at any rate the space, the ability to move and act without prior negotiation with anyone else. It's a space I vigorously defend when it comes up in discussion at, for example, the Tuesday coffee group. The few other singles are widowers and widowed and are weathering the effect of their spouse's premature or sudden death. It is generally assumed that they will find another partner as soon as a decent period of – say six months – has passed. People are beginning to playfully wonder when I am going to find someone: recent advice was to frequent supermarkets more and use the internet. I might! Meanwhile I notice that the low days are never for more than a day and always seem to be followed by very productive days. Something may, I hope, be being processed on the off days that I am not conscious of. Best I find simply to observe as best one can and give it some but not too much attention.

*   *   *   *   *   *   *

Just before returning, I was invited for *apéritifs* to the home of a retired Dutch couple. They had a converted farmhouse on a beautiful site, a little up a valley with an orchard, a wood, a pond area with a bridge and some lovely old fir trees. They explained that in the 15 months they had been there, they had had some of the slope dug out to create a large outside area which they had had covered with a sturdy oak verandah. There was still much to do they assured me. Johann asked me what my feelings were about being in the UK and here. He knew I was keeping my options open for a couple of years or so. What I said was

'The quality of life here is infinitely better'.

There was a 'but' in my voice which I did not elaborate on nor did I explain the 'infinitely better'. I tried to explain it to myself later. The 'but' is all the little attachments of a lifetime elsewhere, and my apartment in Devon of which I am fond. The 'infinitely better' is the air quality, the climate, the drinking water, the rubbish being collected three times a week, shopping in the village and the village markets, the excellent health service, the delicious home grown produce, interesting encounters, the splendid palaces I visit for a coffee or an aperitif, the possibility of skiing in the winter and swimming in the Atlantic in the summer, the lack of spin, the long lunch breaks and – yes – the **lack** of French bureaucracy. Things work. Most of all I notice a gentle playful side of myself brought out by being here. I notice it because every so often I have to ring to sort out something in England and after going through several expensive numbers and their time-wasting menus, I finally reach a young robotic voice who as often as not incorrectly brings up my details on her computer by which time I am seething, abrupt, brusque and rigidly business like.

I made a further acquaintance – a precious one with the *veterinaire*'s wife. We had sat next to each other at the Hundred Year's War lecture and established that we both came from the same village. I wanted to get to know her and hoped that our paths would cross at some stage which they did – in the village paper shop. I went to her house for coffee and she came to mine for tea the day before I was due to leave. We planned reciprocal French and English lessons and to go out to events together in September on my return.

7

Little by little

I was as before a little reluctant to return to France. Life continued apace back home and a long stretch in France seemed a scary void. I was reluctant to separate from my son again though each leaving was easier than the previous one. I had moreover 'met' someone. Despite my assertion about liking being alone made to the coffee group wags, or possibly as a result of their encouragement I had gone on the net and made contact with Simon who though my age and technically retired had a number of work commitments (as well as family commitments) in the UK.

I was not however separating from my cat. He had been in a sorry state when I returned at the beginning of the summer. The vet explained this by an overactive thyroid for which there were pills, and fleas. Didn't they take a while and much hard work to sort? I am no expert on cat psychology but it seemed like he had lost the will to live. He spent the day under a chest of drawers behind some cake tins venturing forth only a few feet to the litter tray or his food. Over the summer months, he was coaxed out and occupied the kitchen table (normally strictly forbidden.) Again he was persuaded onto a side table in his own Argus rabbit cage which he occupied regally at a vantage point able to observe anyone approaching up or down. Finally he took to straddling my desk to which I frequently returned in search of papers. In this sorry state he was visited by well wishers and neighbours who had known him in his better days and it was predicted that he was near the end. It was clear that I could not leave him behind but I delayed making the copious and expensive arrangements to take him with me so that we got away a little later in September than I had planned. This of course did not matter at all in the greater scheme of things. I could not persuade anyone to accompany us on the car journey partly because I put them off by warning them that it would be awful – which it was. I doubted he would survive – which he did. He was too old for tranquillisers the vet said. When he wasn't being sick, he spent the journey under the accelerator, or on my lap but fortunately when we were routinely stopped by the gendarmes he was in his basket. I broke the journey to give my nerves a break at the *auberge* I had happened on when travelling back to the UK in the summer.

Vendôme is a soothing town with some magnificent monuments and easy shopping where I bought an M and S tee shirt as it was warmer than I had anticipated. Maimai concealed himself under the bed. Driving through Normandy in the midday was uncomfortably hot so I planned to have a long midday break on the second day. This proved to be unnecessary as the tail end of a tornado hit the auto route and I was lashed with rain which made for cooler if unideal driving conditions. And so we arrived gratefully to my little house and settled in once more.

This time was for a good six months – driven by UK regs for re-entering pets. This meant winter in France. This meant winterising the house and the longest stretch yet. On the plus side I hoped to improve my French and also to sample the Pyrenean landscape and winter sports. I also intended to go in search of English teaching and get established.

The first few weeks were very long. I started to ration my reading as I had several good books – albeit to last for many months – and I was resorting to reading instead of 'getting on with things'. However, as I always tell myself on returning from the UK, I need to have a bit of a recovery period – a holiday. It had been very hectic in the summer – no time to read at all or think. I had taken on some crap cleaning job in the morning and also at times some TEFL teaching with teenagers in the afternoon. Not infrequently I was up to midnight preparing lessons. Then there was sorting out the house and a new tenant plus the journey. The books I read turned out to be all of a dark genre in the first person, death by aids, etc. Not until some weeks later I started 'Letters of Love' by Niall Ferguson did reading lift the spirits. I was also confused about my sudden connection with the new man. On the face of it we knew little about each other – an internet profile followed by two very harmonious afternoons eating and touring charity shops in Taunton and yet in some mysterious way I knew we were right for each other. We had decided given the practicalities that we would see where we each were the following April. Yet I knew exactly where I would be – I would be where I was now.

There were teething problems getting an internet connection and I panicked when my phone crackled off. These minutiae of a normal life plus sorting out a gap in the chimney breast, tuiles on the roof, and researching insulation, I can see in retrospect prevented launching into teaching, writing or whatever. It is only now after another returning (a week in the UK seeing my son off to the Alps for the fourth year running and a new tenant in) that I feel (mid-Dec) I can let the practicalities go until the next tile springs a leak at least. At the time, however, my lack of productivity seemed to my inner critic, a grave tendency to procrastinate and something I did not want to demonstrate in my not infrequent email contact with the new man. Tactfully he left off asking what success I had in contacting the local school in search of a teaching slot. I suppose I began yet again to feel very split. One part of me was planning an independent future and yet I was pursuing a second not so independent path at the same time. This process of pursuing two paths simultaneously is something that seems almost inevitable when contemplating change. It's very tiring and the impulse to integration takes a while to evolve into a solution.

In fact during those early weeks, things were building up socially. The French classes were rearranged due to one of the teachers having a baby and I found myself in the advanced class to which a near neighbour also went. She and her husband – escapees from Germany – had been in the area for a year and were very content with their new retired existence. The vet's wife who I had met at the end of my summer stay introduced me to a French walking group. This meets twice a week.

'I will collect you at 7.20' Sylvie said. My usual tactic when something is unclear or odd is to ask contextual questions-

'Will it be dark?'

'Yes'

'Is it before breakfast?'

'Yes'

So the next morning I set the alarm for an hour earlier and hoped I had understood aright.

We walked out under the stars and watched the sun rise. It was a beautiful experience and one I have repeated often since. It also became a time to learn more French and in some cases to teach English. One walk was spent discussing my wish to teach or need to generate some income. One person thought it should be done legally and expensively whilst another was keen that I get on and do it. The thought of transgressing all the same sort of rules that exist in England fed into my nervousness. Should I have a police check? How did I fit in with French insurance regs ? I didn't do it.

I was invited around several times by a couple who lived a little way away and on some flimsy pretext wined and dined me. I enjoyed very much working in their garden. There was much to do at that time of year and as often as not the weather was gorgeous. Having virtually no outdoor space myself it was always a treat to go there.

Patricia's family accepted me as a sort of surrogate aunt, I enjoyed very much being with the children, shared meals and some reciprocity Her husband did the odd DIY job and I did l baby/child sitting occasionally.

The cat settled down very well. He remained a house cat but ventured forth from time to time to the yard where there was a supply of rain water which he preferred. He was curious about the front door leading onto the main road which I let him explore at dead of night when a stray lorry or two coming up from Spain sent him scurrying back in.

He had his favourite sleeping arrangements but varied them in a spontaneous way like he always used to. A friend who had seen him in the summer and came out to visit couldn't believe it was the same animal. After a month we ventured out in the car once more for his blood test to establish that he had built up the required level of rabies immunity for returning to the UK in April. This was traumatic for both of us, necessitated a general anaesthetic and overall cost 200 euros. I was very thrown when the results came back from the authorised laboratory and his immunity was half what it needed to be. Was he ever going back? Sometime much later when I had calmed down and been recommended another vet who knew another cheaper laboratory we went through the process again. This time it was over in minutes. I held him whilst the blood was drawn from his neck and apart from the longer car journey and an evening of sulking, he was soon himself again and I was only 80 euros poorer. I had no idea what the future would be or whether I would be able to spare him the journey to and fro but I needed the option of bringing him back.

My neighbour – Maggie – had unfortunately fallen ill during the summer and I spent some time with her. Then I branched out into entertaining. I had two dinner parties using every item of crockery and cutlery I possessed supplemented by paper plates for the four plus courses that are de rigeur here. I also had two visitors to stay. Both came for only a few days and took most of that time to wind down after their UK pace. We fitted in one or two visits and one or two eatings out. But it was all too short. My easiest visitor was a cat sitter I imported from my home town. He was a young painter and I had admired his paintings in a local show but said that there was no way I could afford them … however if he was interested I had a house in France where he might like to stay. Time went by, he was busy with commissions but expressed an interest in coming out to paint and I expressed a need for a cat sitter. Happily the arrangement worked perfectly for us both. He came a day or so early so that I could show him around and I enjoyed learning how it is for a young person making it in the art world. Then I took off.

As my week in the UK approached, things came to a head with Simon. It seemed important that we meet after what was becoming more romantic and binding – a few letters which we both treasured and in which we expressed out longings and ideas abut relationships: long weekly phone calls where we shared whatever came into our heads and daily emails– something of a mundane journal. Yet it seemed difficult to timetable in more than a quick exchange over one night and following morning in the week of my UK stay. In the end my son took off earlier than he had planned to do and Simon chose to end or at least re-jig another relationship which was getting in the way. So we ended up on firmer ground after spending a couple of days together. We agreed to give it a go with as yet no commitment sort of engagement. All this was very absorbing and exciting and overshadowed all else as in my case there was not much else going on. The theme of this time then became a lesson in how to retain my own sense of direction and not become totally absorbed in someone else's life amidst an overwhelming emotional desire to be close. I was amused to see how little had changed in forming this new relationship from the way I had become absorbed in earlier times. This time, however, it seemed more mutual.

The week of my return to France was the weekend of the Telethon – an annual fundraising event on a par with Children in Need. The Brits of Trie were specifically asked to run an event based on a hugely successful Quiz night the previous year.

I went with a friend into the crowded café enlarged for the event by a well-constructed extra 'room' – a tarpaulin enclosed area of the outside pavement. Conversation with the other people on our table – two sisters who finding themselves alone had joined forces – the one from a life in Denmark and the other from up North in the UK – was limited given the noise level and country music live band. It was something to be endured rather than enjoyed which seems a bit churlish considering the enormous work involved by the organisers who with the aid of a tombola raised 1700 plus euros. The questions were in both French and English and we were limited by our lack of knowledge on the sports section. Ah well – we all seem to have emerged with more than we brought! I had a Credit Agricole umbrella and a Haute Pyrenees tee shirt. (There were eighty prizes garnered from the local businesses.)

The year was drawing to a close. I was delighted by the local Christmas decorations which appeared in the second week of December. The street light suspended from my house on a curly bracket with a flourish had been adorned with a sort of cockade made from a string of lights – white on my side of the road and green on the other. The lampposts were coiled with the same strings. It seemed modest and tasteful. Just as I was savouring this restraint compared with the ghastly chaos back in the UK the Petit Marmite exploded with grotesque inflatable figures on swathes of white cloth with an annoying musical accompaniment. Was this a joke or what?

I was curious to know how Noël would be. Should I send cards to my neighbours and if so when? For Christmas day itself, Patricia had invited me to join her family. I took up the invitation to join them for tea and headed out during the day to the mountains. Little did I know this was to become an oft repeated habit – a trip to Cauterets about an hour and a half away. Cauterets is not itself very high but there is a cable car to a mid-point restaurant where I watched the skiers whilst chomping on my lasagne. My one regret was that I had no-one to go to the New Year *Saint- Sylvestre Bal Musette* with. But then Simon came to the rescue.

Glossary

Auberge   *local restaurant and/ or hotel*

Apéritifs   *early evening drinks and nibbles*

Bal Musette *a very common dance night much beloved by the older generation*

Bastide   *fortified mediaeval village structured around a square*

Cave   *cellar (often a wine store)*

Chambre d'hôte *bed and breakfast*

Compostella *way one of the many pilgrim routes leading to Santiago in Spain*

Cuisinaire   *combined cooker and wood burning stove*

Garbure   *soup which is a meal in itself with meat and cabbage.*

Gite   *catering accommodation*

Notaire   *lawer*

Propriétaire *owner*

Saisonnière *someone who works just for the season*

Saint Sylvestre *December 31st is the day of Saint Sylvestre*

Valloné   *with valleys: going up and down*

Vide Grenier *car-boot sale (literally empty the attic)*